P

Use of guidance

THE APPROVED DOCUMENTS

This document is one of a series that has been approved and issued by the Secretary of State for the purpose of providing practical guidance with respect to the requirements of Schedule 1 to and regulation 7 of the Building Regulations 2000 (SI 2000/2531) for England and Wales. SI 2000/2531 has been amended by the Building (Amendment) Regulations 2001 (SI 2001/3335), the Building (Amendment) Regulations 2002 (SI 2002/440), the Building (Amendment) (No 2) Regulations 2002 (SI 2002/2871), the Building (Amendment) Regulations 2003 (SI 2003/2692), the Building (Amendment) Regulations 2004 (SI 2004/1465) and the Building (Amendment) (No 3) Regulations 2004 (SI 2004/3210) and the Building and Approved Inspectors (Amendment) Regulations 2006 (SI 2006/652).

At the back of this document is a list of all the documents that have been approved and issued by the Secretary of State for this purpose.

Approved Documents are intended to provide guidance for some of the more common building situations. However, there may well be alternative ways of achieving compliance with the requirements. **Thus there is no obligation to adopt any particular solution contained in an Approved Document if you prefer to meet the relevant requirement in some other way.**

Supplementary guidance

The Office of the Deputy Prime Minister occasionally issues additional material to aid interpretation of the guidance contained in Approved Documents. This material may be conveyed in official letters to Chief Executives of Local Authorities and Approved Inspectors and/or posted on the websites accessed through: http://www.odpm.gov.uk/building-regulations.

Other requirements

The guidance contained in an Approved Document relates only to the particular requirements of the Regulations which the document addresses. The building work will also have to comply with any other relevant requirements in Schedule 1 to the Regulations.

There are Approved Documents which give guidance on each of the Parts of Schedule 1 and on Regulation 7.

LIMITATION ON REQUIREMENTS

In accordance with regulation 8, the requirements in Parts A to D, F to K, N and P (except for paragraphs H2 and J6) of Schedule 1 to the Building Regulations do not require anything to be done except for the purpose of securing reasonable standards of health and safety for persons in or about buildings (and any others who may be affected by buildings or matters connected with buildings). This is one of the categories of purpose for which Building Regulations may be made.

Paragraphs H2 and J6 are excluded from regulation 8 because they deal directly with prevention of the contamination of water. Parts E and M (which deal, respectively, with resistance to the passage of sound, and access to and use of buildings) are excluded from regulation 8 because they address the welfare and convenience of building users. Part L is excluded from regulation 8 because it addresses the conservation of fuel and power. All these matters are amongst the purposes, other than health and safety, that may be addressed by Building Regulations.

MATERIALS AND WORKMANSHIP

Any building work which is subject to the requirements imposed by Schedule 1 to the Building Regulations should, in accordance with regulation 7, be carried out with proper materials and in a workmanlike manner.

You may show that you have complied with regulation 7 in a number of ways. These include the appropriate use of a product bearing CE marking in accordance with the Construction Products Directive (89/106/EEC)[1], the Low Voltage Directive (73/23/EEC and amendment 93/68/EEC)[2] and the EMC Directive (89/336/ EEC)[3], as amended by the CE marking Directive (93/68/EEC)[4], or a product complying with an appropriate technical specification (as defined in those Directives), a British Standard, or an alternative national technical specification of any state which is a contracting party to the European Economic Area which, in use, is equivalent, or a product covered by a national or European certificate issued by a European Technical Approval issuing body, and the conditions of use are in accordance with the terms of the certificate. You will find further guidance in the Approved Document supporting regulation 7 on materials and workmanship.

---

[1] As implemented by the Construction Products Regulations 1991 (SI 1620/1991).

[2] As implemented by the Electrical Equipment (Safety) Regulations 1994 (SI 3260/1994).

[3] As implemented by the Electromagnetic Compatibility Regulations 1992 (SI 2372/1992).

[4] As implemented by the Construction Products (Amendment) Regulations 1994 (SI 3051/1994) and the Electromagnetic Compatibility (Amendment) Regulations 1994 (SI 3080/1994).

Independent certification schemes

There are many UK product certification schemes. Such schemes certify compliance with the requirements of a recognised document which is appropriate to the purpose for which the material is to be used. Materials which are not so certified may still conform to a relevant standard.

Many certification bodies which approve such schemes are accredited by UKAS.

Technical specifications

Under section 1(1) of the Building Act 1984, Building Regulations may be made for various purposes including health, safety, welfare, convenience, conservation of fuel and power and prevention of waste or contamination of water, furthering the protection or enhancement of the environment, facilitating sustainable development or the prevention and detection of crime. Standards and technical approvals are relevant guidance to the extent that they relate to these considerations. However, they may also address other aspects of performance such as serviceability, or aspects which, although they relate to the purposes listed above, are not covered by the current Regulations.

When an Approved Document makes reference to a named standard, the relevant version of the standard is the one listed at the end of the publication. However, if this version has been revised or updated by the issuing standards body, the new version may be used as a source of guidance provided it continues to address the relevant requirements of the Regulations.

The appropriate use of a product which complies with a European Technical Approval as defined in the Construction Products Directive will meet the relevant requirements.

The Office intends to issue periodic amendments to its Approved Documents to reflect emerging harmonised European Standards. Where a national standard is to be replaced by a European harmonised standard, there will be a co-existence period during which either standard may be referred to. At the end of the co-existence period the national standard will be withdrawn.

MIXED USE DEVELOPMENT

In mixed use developments part of a building may be used as a dwelling while another part has a non-domestic use. In such cases, if the requirements of the Regulations for dwellings and non-domestic use differ, the requirements for non-domestic use should apply in any shared parts of the building.

THE WORKPLACE (HEALTH, SAFETY AND WELFARE) REGULATIONS 1992

The Workplace (Health, Safety and Welfare) Regulations 1992 as amended contain some requirements which affect building design. The main requirements are now covered by the Building Regulations, but for further information see: *Workplace health, safety and welfare: Workplace (Health, Safety and Welfare) Regulations 1992, Approved Code of Practice*, L24, HMSO, 1992 (ISBN 0 7176 0413 6).

The Workplace (Health, Safety and Welfare) Regulations 1992 apply to the common parts of flats and similar buildings if people such as cleaners and caretakers are employed to work in these common parts. Where the requirements of the Building Regulations that are covered by this Part do not apply to buildings other than dwellings, the provisions may still be required in the situations described above in order to satisfy the Workplace Regulations.

Contents

The Requirements

This Approved Document, which takes effect on
6 April 2006, deals with the requirements of Part P
of Schedule 1 to the Building Regulations 2000
(as amended by SI 2004/3210 and SI 2006/652).

Requirement	Limits on application
PART P ELECTRICAL SAFETY **Design and installation** **P1.** Reasonable provision shall be made in the design and installation of electrical installations in order to protect persons operating, maintaining or altering the installations from fire or injury.	The requirements of this part apply only to electrical installations that are intended to operate at low or extra-low voltage and are: (a) in or attached to a dwelling; (b) in the common parts of a building serving one or more dwellings, but excluding power supplies to lifts; (c) in a building that receives its electricity from a source located within or shared with a dwelling; and (d) in a garden or in or on land associated with a building where the electricity is from a source located within or shared with a dwelling.

NOTES

Examples of application of Part P

Part P applies to electrical installations in or attached to buildings or parts of buildings comprising:

- dwelling houses and flats;

- dwellings and business premises that have a common supply – for example shops and public houses with a flat above;

- common access areas in blocks of flats such as corridors and staircases;

- shared amenities of blocks of flats such as laundries and gymnasiums.

Part P applies also to parts of the above electrical installations:

- in or on land associated with the buildings – for example Part P applies to fixed lighting and pond pumps in gardens;

- in outbuildings such as sheds, detached garages and greenhouses.

Interaction with other Parts of the Building Regulations

Other Parts of Schedule 1 to the Building Regulations contain requirements affecting electrical installations. Examples include, but are not limited to:

- Part A (Structure): depth of chases in walls, and size of holes and notches in floor and roof joists;

- Part B (Fire safety): fire safety of certain electrical installations; provision of fire alarm and fire detection systems; fire resistance of penetrations through floors and walls;

- Part C (Site preparation and resistance to moisture): moisture resistance of cable penetrations through external walls;

- Part E (Resistance to the passage of sound): penetrations through floors and walls;

- Part L (Conservation of fuel and power): energy efficient lighting; reduced current-carrying capacity of cables in insulation;

- Part M (Access to and use of buildings): height of socket outlets, switches and consumer units.

Further guidance is available in:

- the *Electrician's guide to the Building Regulations*, published by the IEE (Institution of Electrical Engineers), available from www.iee.org

- the *Electrical Installers' Guide to the Building Regulations* published by the NICEIC Group Limited and the ECA (Electrical Contractors' Association), available from www.niceic.org.uk or www.eca.co.uk.

Regulation 4(2) states that, on completion of electrical installation work, the building (and parts of the electrical installations in the building that were not the subject of work) should be no worse in terms of the level of compliance with the other applicable Parts of Schedule 1 to the Building Regulations than before the work was undertaken.

For example, one or more perforations of a ceiling lining beneath a floor – made to accommodate recessed lighting or similar fittings – may have an adverse effect on that floor's performance in terms of its resistance to fire and sound penetration. Due regard should therefore be paid to the guidance in Approved Documents B and E on the performance of compartment floors.

Regulation 4(2) also means that, when extending or altering an installation, only the new work must meet current requirements and there is no obligation to upgrade the existing installation unless the new work would adversely affect the safety of the existing installation, or the state of the existing installation was such that the new work could not be operated safely, or where there is a requirement to upgrade imposed by the energy efficiency requirements of the Building Regulations.

Section 0: General guidance

Performance

0.1 In the Secretary of State's view, the requirements will be met by adherence to the 'Fundamental Principles' for achieving safety given in BS 7671:2001 Chapter 13. To achieve these requirements electrical installations must be:

a. designed and installed to afford appropriate protection against mechanical and thermal damage, and so that they do not present electric shock and fire hazards to people;

b. suitably inspected and tested to verify that they meet the relevant equipment and installation standards.

General

0.2 A way of satisfying the fundamental principles would be to follow:

a. the technical rules described in the body of BS 7671:2001 as amended or in an equivalent standard approved by a member of the EEA; and

b. guidance given in installation manuals that are consistent with BS 7671:2001, such as:

   i. the IEE (Institution of Electrical Engineers) On-Site Guide;

   ii. the series of IEE Publications, Guidance Notes Nos 1 to 7.

0.3 The diagrams in Appendix A give an indication of the sorts of electrical services encountered in dwellings, some of the ways they can be connected and the complexity of the wiring and protective systems necessary to supply them. **They are not an indication of the scope of Part P and must not be used for installation purposes.**

Definitions

0.4 The following meanings apply throughout this document:

Electrical installation is defined in the Building Regulations as fixed electrical cables or fixed electrical equipment located on the consumer's side of the electricity supply meter.

Extra-low voltage is defined in the Building Regulations as voltage not exceeding 50 volts between conductors and earth for alternating current or 120 volts between conductors for direct current.

Low voltage which normally exceeds extra-low voltage is defined in the Building Regulations as not exceeding 1000 volts between conductors or 600 volts between conductors and earth for alternating current; or 1500 volts between conductors or 900 volts between conductors and earth for direct current.

Kitchen is defined in the Building Regulations as 'a room or part of a room which contains a sink and food preparation facilities'.

As a guide only, in open plan areas the zone of a kitchen may be considered to extend from the edge of the sink to a distance of 3m or to a nearer dividing wall.

Other Regulations

0.5 Electrical work is also affected by the Electricity at Work Regulations 1989 as amended and the Electricity Safety, Quality and Continuity Regulations 2002 as amended, as described in paragraphs 3.1 to 3.13.

Notification of work

When necessary to involve building control bodies

0.6 Except in the circumstances outlined in paragraph 0.7 below, notification of proposals to carry out electrical installation work must be given to a building control body (the local authority or an approved inspector) before work begins.

When not necessary to involve building control bodies

0.7 It is not necessary to give prior notification of proposals to carry out electrical installation work to building control bodies in the following circumstances:

a. The proposed installation work is undertaken by a person registered with an electrical self-certification scheme prescribed in regulations (see schedule 2A of the Regulations). In these cases the person is responsible for ensuring compliance with BS 7671:2001 or an equivalent standard and all relevant building regulations requirements. A full list of schemes with contact details is given in Appendix E.

OR

b. The proposed electrical installation work is non-notifiable work of the type described in Table 1 and does not include the provision of a new circuit (see schedule 2B of the Regulations).

Table 1 **Work that need not be notified to building control bodies**

Work consisting of:

Replacing any fixed electrical equipment (for example, socket-outlets, control switches and ceiling roses) which does not include the provision of any new fixed cabling

Replacing the cable for a single circuit only, where damaged, for example, by fire, rodent or impact [a]

Re-fixing or replacing the enclosures of existing installation components [b]

Providing mechanical protection to existing fixed installations [c]

Installing or upgrading main or supplementary equipotential bonding [d]

Work that is not in a kitchen or special location and does not involve a special installation[e] and consists of:

Adding lighting points (light fittings and switches) to an existing circuit [f]

Adding socket-outlets and fused spurs to an existing ring or radial circuit [f]

Work not in a special location, on:

Telephone or extra-low voltage wiring and equipment for the purposes of communications, information technology, signalling, control and similar purposes

Prefabricated equipment sets and associated flexible leads with integral plug and socket connections

Notes:

(a)   On condition that the replacement cable has the same current-carrying capacity and follows the same route.

(b)   If the circuit's protective measures are unaffected.

(c)   If the circuit's protective measures and current-carrying capacity of conductors are unaffected by increased thermal insulation.

(d)   Such work will need to comply with other applicable legislation, such as the Gas Safety (Installation and Use) Regulations.

(e)   Special locations and installations are listed in Table 2.

(f)   Only if the existing circuit protective device is suitable and provides protection for the modified circuit, and other relevant safety provisions are satisfactory.

Table 2 **Special locations and installations[a]**

Special locations

Locations containing a bath tub or shower basin
Swimming pools or paddling pools
Hot air saunas

Special installations

Electric floor or ceiling heating systems
Garden lighting or power installations
Solar photovoltaic (PV) power supply systems
Small scale generators such as microCHP units
Extra-low voltage lighting installations, other than pre-assembled, CE-marked lighting sets

Note:

(a)   See IEE Guidance Note 7 which gives more guidance on achieving safe installations where risks to people are greater.

Additional notes

Tables 1 and 2 above give the general rules for determining whether or not electrical installation work is notifiable. The rules are based on the risk of fire and injury and what is practicable. The following notes provide additional guidance and specific examples:

a.   Notifiable jobs include new circuits back to the consumer unit, and extensions to circuits in kitchens and special locations (bathrooms, etc) and associated with special installations (garden lighting and power installations, etc).

b.   Replacement, repair and maintenance jobs are generally not notifiable, even if carried out in a kitchen or special location or associated with a special installation.

c.   Consumer unit replacements are, however, notifiable.

d.   In large bathrooms, the location containing a bath or shower is defined by the walls of the bathroom.

e.   Conservatories and attached garages are not special locations. Work in them is therefore not notifiable unless it involves the installation of a new circuit or the extension of a circuit in a kitchen or special location or associated with a special installation.

f.   Detached garages and sheds are not special locations. Work within them is notifiable only if it involves new outdoor wiring.

g. Outdoor lighting and power installations are special installations. Any new work in, for example, the garden or that involves crossing the garden is notifiable.

h. The installation of fixed equipment is within the scope of Part P, even where the final connection is by a 13A plug and socket. However, work is notifiable only if it involves fixed wiring and the installation of a new circuit or the extension of a circuit in a kitchen or special location or associated with a special installation.

i. The installation of equipment attached to the outside wall of a house (for example security lighting, air conditioning equipment and radon fans) is not notifiable provided that there are no exposed outdoor connections and the work does not involve the installation of a new circuit or the extension of a circuit in a kitchen or special location or associated with a special installation.

j. The installation of a socket outlet on an external wall is notifiable, since the socket outlet is an outdoor connector that could be connected to cables that cross the garden and requires RCD protection.

k. The installation of prefabricated, "modular" systems (for example kitchen lighting systems and armoured garden cabling) linked by plug and socket connectors is not notifiable, provided that products are CE-marked and that any final connections in kitchens and special locations are made to existing connection units or points (possibly a 13A socket outlet).

l. Work to connect an electric gate or garage door to an existing isolator is not notifiable, but installation of the circuit up to the isolator is notifiable.

m. The fitting and replacement of cookers and electric showers is not notifiable unless a new circuit is needed.

n. New central heating control wiring installations are notifiable even where work in kitchens and bathrooms is avoided.

Section 1: Design, installation, inspection and testing, and provision of information

General

1.1 Where electrical installation work is to be carried out professionally, compliance is necessary with the Electricity at Work Regulations 1989 as amended.

1.2 In accordance with the Electricity Safety, Quality and Continuity Regulations 2002 and the contract for a mains supply, proposals for new installations of a mains supply or significant alterations to an existing mains supply must be agreed with the electricity distributor.

Design and installation

General

1.3 Electrical installations should be designed and constructed, suitably enclosed and separated by appropriate distances to provide mechanical and thermal protection, so that they afford appropriate protection for persons against the risks of electric shock, burn or fire injuries.

1.4 A way of complying is to follow the technical rules in BS 7671:2001 as amended or an equivalent standard.

Protection against flooding

1.5 The Electricity Safety, Quality and Continuity Regulations 2002 require the electricity distributor to install the cut-out and meter in a safe location, where they are mechanically protected and can be safely maintained. In compliance with this requirement, the electricity distributor and installer may be required to take into account the risk of flooding. Some guidance is given in the ODPM publication *Preparing for flooding*, available from www.odpm.gov.uk.

Accessibility

1.6 Wall-mounted socket outlets, switches and consumer units should be located so that they are easily reachable where this is necessary to comply with Part M of the Building Regulations. Approved Document M shows ways of complying. Accessible consumer units should comply with BS EN 60439-3.

Inspection and testing before taking into service

General

1.7 Electrical installations should be inspected and tested as necessary and appropriate during and at the end of installation, before they are taken into service, to verify that they are safe to use, maintain and alter and comply with Part P of the Building Regulations and with any other relevant Parts of the Building Regulations.

BS 7671 installation certificates

1.8 In general, compliance with Part P can be demonstrated by the issue of the appropriate BS 7671 electrical installation certificate.

1.9 Inspection and testing should be carried out to follow the procedures in Chapters 71 and 74 of BS 7671:2001, and a copy of the appropriate installation certificate should be supplied to the person ordering the work. The electrical installation certificate must be made out and signed only by someone "qualified" to do so. Where this is the case, a safety certificate should be issued for all but the simplest of like-for-like replacements.

1.10 "Qualified" in this context means having the appropriate qualifications, knowledge and experience to carry out the inspection and testing procedures and complete the relevant electrical installation certificate.

1.11 The certificate should show that the electrical installation work has been:

a. Inspected appropriately during erection as well as on completion to verify that the components are:

  i. made in compliance with appropriate British Standards or harmonised European Standards;

  ii. selected and installed in accordance with BS 7671:2001 (including consideration of external influences such as the presence of moisture);

  iii. not visibly damaged or defective so as to be unsafe.

b. Tested appropriately to check satisfactory performance in relation to continuity of conductors, insulation resistance, separation of circuits, polarity, earthing and bonding arrangements, earth fault loop impedance and functionality of all protective devices including residual current devices. It is not necessary to carry out all these tests for each and every installation, only those which are needed to establish whether the installation is safe.

1.12 Appendix 6 of BS 7671 and Appendix B of this Approved Document contain models of the various BS 7671 certificates. Qualified installers should use the one appropriate to the work they have carried out.

1.13 BS 7671 does not insist on a Minor Works Certificate being issued for the replacement of equipment such as accessories or luminaires, but advises that this should be done where appropriate inspection and testing has been carried out, irrespective of the extent of the work undertaken. The Minor Works Certificate is **not** appropriate for the replacement of consumer units or similar items, for which the full Electrical Installation Certificate should be used.

1.14 Section 712 of BS 7671:2001 provides a list of all the inspections that may be necessary although in particular cases only some elements will be relevant. A schedule of inspections forms part of the Electrical Installation Certificate in Appendix 6 of BS 7671 and in this Approved Document at Appendix B.

1.15 Section 713 of BS 7671:2001 provides a list of all the tests that may be necessary although, again, in particular cases only some elements may be relevant. A blank schedule for recording test results also forms part of the Electrical Installation Certificate. Tests should be carried out using appropriate and accurate instruments under the conditions given in BS 7671, and the results compared with the relevant performance criteria to confirm compliance.

1.16 The Minor Works Certificate lists six essential tests for additions and alterations that do not include the provision of a new circuit. Appropriate tests should be carried out depending on the nature of the work.

Building Regulations compliance certificates/ notices for notifiable work

1.17 A Building Regulations compliance certificate (issued by Part P competent person scheme installers), completion certificates (issued by local authorities) and final notices (issued by approved inspectors) are evidence that compliance with the Building Regulations has been achieved, and are issued on completion of notifiable works only. They are different documents than a BS 7671 installation certificate and attest compliance with all relevant requirements of the Building Regulations, not just Part P.

Certification of notifiable work

a. *Where the installer is registered with a Part P competent person self-certification scheme*

1.18 Installers registered with a Part P competent person self-certification scheme are qualified to complete BS 7671 installation certificates and should do so in respect of every job they undertake. A copy of the certificate should always be given to the person ordering the electrical installation work.

1.19 Where installers registered with Part P competent person self-certification scheme, a Building Regulations compliance certificate must be issued to the occupant either by the installer or the installer's registration body within 30 days of the work being completed. The relevant building control body should also receive a copy of the information on the certificate within 30 days.

1.20 The Regulations call for the Building Regulations compliance certificate to be issued to the occupier. However, in the case of rented properties, the certificate may be sent to the person ordering the work with a copy sent also to the occupant.

b. *Where the installer is not registered with a Part P competent person self-certification scheme but qualified to complete BS 7671 installation certificates*

1.21 Where notifiable electrical installer work is carried out by a person not registered with a Part P competent person self-certification the work should be notified to a building control body (the local authority or an approved inspector) before work starts. Where the work is necessary because of an emergency the building control body should be notified as soon as possible. The building control body becomes responsible for making sure the work is safe and complies with all relevant requirements of the Building Regulations.

1.22 Where installers are qualified to carry out inspection and testing and completing the appropriate BS 7671 installation certificate, they should do so. A copy of the certificate should then be given to the building control body. The building control body will take this certificate into account in deciding what further action (if any) needs to be taken to make sure that the work is safe and complies fully with all relevant requirements. Building control bodies may ask for evidence that installers are qualified in this case.

1.23 Where the building control body decides that the work is safe and meets all building regulation requirements it will issue a building regulation completion certificate (the local authority) on request or a final certificate (an approved inspector).

c. *Where installers are not qualified to complete BS 7671 completion certificates*

1.24 Where such installers (who may be contractors or DIYers) carry out notifiable electrical work, the building control body must be notified before the work starts. Where the work is necessary because of an emergency the building control body should be notified as soon as possible. The building control body then becomes responsible for making sure that the work is safe and complies with all relevant requirements in the Building Regulations.

1.25 The amount of inspection and testing needed is for the building control body to decide, based on the nature and extent of the electrical work. For relatively simple notifiable jobs, such as adding a socket-outlet to a kitchen circuit, the inspection and testing requirements will be minimal. For a house re-wire, a full set of inspections and tests may need to be carried out.

1.26 The building control body may choose to carry out the inspection and testing itself, or to contract out some or all of the work to a specialist body which will then carry out the work on its behalf. Building control bodies will carry out the necessary inspection and testing at their expense, not at the householders' expense.

1.27 A building control body will **not** issue a BS 7671 installation certificate (as these can be issued only by those carrying out the work), but only a Building Regulations completion certificate (the local authority) or a final certificate (an approved inspector).

Third party certification

1.28 Unregistered installers should not themselves arrange for a third party to carry out final inspection and testing. The third party – not having supervised the work from the outset – would not be in a position to verify that the installation work complied fully with BS 7671:2001 requirements. An electrical installation certificate can be issued only by the installer responsible for the installation work.

1.29 A third party could only sign a BS 7671:2001 Periodic Inspection Report or similar. The Report would indicate that electrical safety tests had been carried out on the installation which met BS 7671:2001 criteria, but it could not verify that the installation complied fully with BS 7671:2001 requirements – for example with regard to routing of hidden cables.

Inspection and testing of non-notifiable work

1.30 Non-notifiable electrical installation work must also be carried out in accordance with the requirements of BS 7671:2001 or an equivalent standard. However, it is not necessary for the work to be checked by a building control body or alternatively carried out by an installer registered with a Part P competent person self-certification scheme.

1.31 Local authorities, however, can take enforcement action if non-notifiable work – for example electrical work which is part of a wider project – is found to be unsafe and non-compliant.

1.32 Those qualified to complete BS 7671 installation certificates who carry out non-notifiable work should issue the appropriate electrical installation certificate for all but the simplest of like-for-like replacements. DIYers may wish to employ a qualified third party to carry out inspection and testing of non-notifiable work to make sure it is safe. The qualified person need not necessarily be registered with a Part P competent person self-certification scheme but, as required by BS 7671, must be qualified in respect of the inspection and testing of an installation.

Provision of information

1.33 Sufficient information should be left with the occupant to ensure that persons wishing to operate, maintain or alter an electrical installation can do so with reasonable safety.

1.34 The information should comprise items called for by BS 7671:2001 or an equivalent standard and other appropriate information including:

a. electrical installation certificates describing the installation and giving details of work carried out;

b. permanent labels, for example on earth connections and bonds, and on items of electrical equipment such as consumer units and RCDs;

c. operating instructions and log books;

d. for unusually large or complex installations only, detailed plans.

Section 2: Extensions, material alterations and material changes of use

2.1 Where any electrical installation work is classified as an extension, a material alteration or a material change of use, the addition and alteration work must include:

a. such works on the existing fixed electrical installation in the building as are necessary to enable the additions and alterations, the circuits which feed them, the protective measures and the relevant earthing and bonding systems to meet the requirements; and

b. establishing that the mains supply equipment is suitable.

2.2 A way of complying would be to follow for the new work the guidance given above in Section 1 in relation to design, construction and inspection and testing and to show that for the altered circumstances:

a. the rating and the condition of the existing equipment belonging to both the consumer and to the electricity distributor:

   i. can carry the additional loads being allowed for, or

   ii. are improved so that they can carry the additional loads being allowed for; and

b. the correct protective measures are used; and

c. the earthing and equipotential bonding arrangements are satisfactory.

2.3 In accordance with Regulation 4(2), the whole of the existing installation does not need to be upgraded to current standards, but only to the extent necessary for the new work to meet current standards except where upgrading is required by the energy efficiency requirements of the Building Regulations.

2.4 Appendix C offers guidance on some of the types of older installations that might be encountered in alteration work.

2.5 Appendix D offers guidance on applying the harmonised European cable identification system when making additions and alterations to existing installations.

Section 3: Information about other legislation

Electricity at Work Regulations 1989

3.1 All electrical installations must be accommodated in ways that meet the requirements of the Building Regulations. However electrical installations carried out by persons on whom duties are imposed by the Electricity at Work Regulations 1989 must meet the requirements of those Regulations.

3.2 The advice given below reflects the present state of the Electricity at Work Regulations 1989 following amendments by Statutory Instruments 1996/192, 1997/1993 and 1999/2024.

3.3 Regulation 3 imposes duties on employers, employees and the self-employed. Regulation 3(2)(b) places duties on employees equivalent to those placed on employers and self-employed persons where there are matters within their control.

3.4 The text of the Electricity at Work Regulations and guidance on how to comply with them are contained in the Health and Safety guidance document ' Memorandum of Guidance on the Electricity at Work Regulations 1989 – HSR25 '. Important elements of the Regulations include:

a. The Electricity at Work Regulations require that electrical work is only carried out by persons that are competent to prevent danger and injury while doing it, or who are appropriately supervised (Regulation 16).

b. The Electricity at Work Regulations set general requirements for the design, construction and suitability of equipment for its intended use (Regulations 4(1), 5, 6, 7, 8, 9, 10, 11, 12).

Electricity Safety, Quality and Continuity Regulations 2002

3.5 The Electricity Safety, Quality and Continuity Regulations 2002 (SI 2002/2665) came into force on 31 January 2003. These Regulations replaced the Electricity Supply Regulations 1988 (as amended).

3.6 The Regulations specify safety standards which are aimed at protecting the general public from danger. In addition, the Regulations specify power quality and supply continuity requirements to ensure an efficient and economic electricity supply service for consumers. The Regulations were introduced to improve standards in public safety and to align requirements to modern electricity markets.

3.7 The duty holders are generators, distributors, suppliers, meter operators, consumers and specified persons. Most of the duties apply to distributors who own or operate networks used to supply consumers' installations, street furniture or other networks.

3.8 Amongst other duties, distributors are required to provide an earthing facility for new connections (unless this would be inappropriate for safety reasons), to maintain the supply within defined tolerance limits and to provide certain technical and safety information to consumers to enable them to design their installations.

3.9 Distributors and meter operators must ensure that their equipment on consumers' premises is suitable for its purpose and safe in its particular environment and that the polarity of conductors is clearly indicated.

3.10 The Regulations allow the Secretary of State to issue safety enforcement notices to consumers in circumstances where consumers' installations outside buildings present a danger to the public.

3.11 In relation to 'embedded' generation[5], the Regulations require persons operating 'switched alternative' sources of energy in their installations to prevent a parallel connection occurring with the distributor's network and to comply with BS 7671. Sources of energy that operate in parallel with the distributor's network must meet certain additional safety standards: for example the equipment must not be a source of danger or cause interference with the distributor's network. Persons installing domestic combined heat and power equipment must advise the local distributor of their intentions before or at the time of commissioning the source.

3.12 Distributors are prevented by the Regulations from connecting installations to their networks which do not comply with BS 7671. Other persons may connect installations to distributors' networks provided they obtain the prior consent of the distributor, who may require evidence that the installation complies with BS 7671 and that the connection itself will meet safety and operational requirements. Distributors may disconnect consumers' installations which are a source of danger or cause interference with their networks or other installations.

3.13 Detailed Guidance on the Regulations is available at www.dti.gov.uk/electricity-regulations.

Functionality requirements

3.14 Part P of the Building Regulations makes requirements covering the safety of fixed electrical installations, but does not cover system functionality. The functionality of electrically powered systems such as fire alarm systems, fans and pumps is covered in other Parts of the Building Regulations and other legislation.

---

[5] 'Embedded' generators are those connected to the distribution networks of public electricity suppliers rather than directly to the National Grid. Most CHP and renewable generating stations are embedded.

Appendix A: Examples of electrical installation diagrams

Notes

1. The diagrams do not give all the information needed to achieve compliance with BS 7671, nor do they cover all the electrical services found in dwellings, some of which (e.g. swimming pools and saunas) are subject to special requirements specified in Part 6 of BS 7671:2001. **The diagrams must not be used for installation purposes.**

2. The diagrams are simplified examples of what may be encountered. They are not a substitute for the proper consideration of for instance:

a. Cross-sectional areas (csa) of the phase and neutral conductors of circuits. The minimum csa required by BS 7671 depends on a number of variables, including: type of cable, number of cores, type and nominal current of overcurrent protective device, grouping with other circuits, ambient temperature, contact with thermally insulating materials and circuit length.

b. Cross-sectional areas of protective conductors. BS 7671 contains different rules, involving a number of variables, for determining the minimum csa for each type of protective conductor, including the earthing conductor, circuit protective conductors, main equipotential bonding conductors and supplementary bonding conductors.

c. Types and nominal current ratings of fuses or circuit breakers. These particulars depend on the circuit design current and load characteristics, and need to be co-ordinated with the circuit conductors and with the earth fault loop impedance of the circuit.

d. Types of wiring or wiring system. While PVC insulated and sheathed cables are likely to be suitable for much of the wiring in a typical dwelling, other types of cable may also be necessary. For example, heat-resisting flexible cables are required for the final connections to certain equipment; the cable to the garage or shed, if run underground, is subject to certain requirements; and cables concealed in floors and walls in certain circumstances are required to have an earthed metal covering, be enclosed in steel conduit or have additional mechanical protection.

e. Principles of cable routing. BS 7671 contains criteria for the routing and positioning of cables, so as to give protection against electric shock and fire as a result of mechanical damage to a cable. For example, such criteria are given for cables concealed in walls or buried in the ground.

f. Current ratings of circuits to fixed current-using equipment such as a shower or cooker.

In the above context, diagrams are given as follows:

Diagram 1(a) indicates the many electrical appliances that can be found in the home and how they might be supplied.

Diagram 1(b) indicates earthing and bonding arrangements that can be necessary.

Diagram 2(a) indicates earthing arrangements as might be provided by electricity distributors.

Diagram 2(b) indicates the earthing arrangements as might need to be provided by the consumer.

Key to diagrams

☐	Single pole switch
■	Double pole switch (DPS)
Pull cord	Pull cord
Fused connection unit	Fused connection unit
Fused connection unit with DPS	Fused connection unit with DPS
Not always fitted	Not always fitted
13A socket-outlet	13A socket-outlet
Shaver socket-outlet	Shaver socket-outlet
Light fitting	Light fitting
Protected light fitting	Protected light fitting

Zone around bath or shower (up to 3m above floor and 3m from edge of bath or shower, as defined in BS 7671:2001). This is a 'special location' where supplementary protection is required against the additional risks of injury.

——————— Live and neutral conductors

··················· Circuit protective conductors

– – – – – – – Main equipotential bonding

— — — — — Supplementary equipotential bonding conductors

— — — — — Earthing conductor

Diagram 1(a) **Illustration of the fixed electrical installation that might be commonly encountered in new or upgraded existing dwellings**

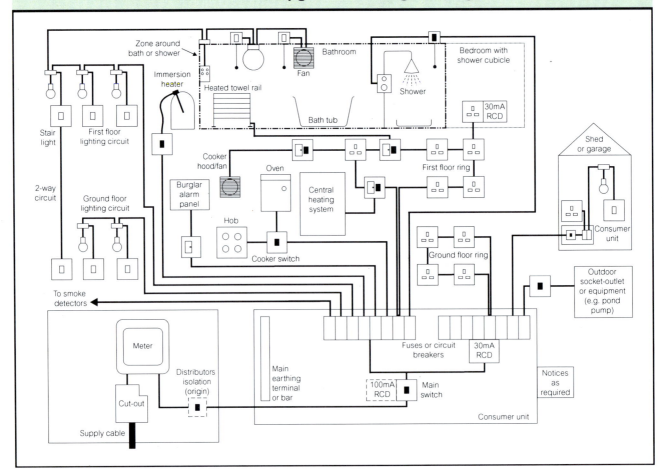

Notes:

1. See the general rules in BS 7671:2001.

2. The RCD component in the main switch is required for TT systems (see Diagram 2(b)). Individual circuit 30mA RCDs may be required to avoid unnecessary tripping.

3. The notices include advice on periodic testing and regular test operation of the RCDs.

4. The zone shown around the bath or shower corresponds to zone 3 in Section 601 of BS 7671:2001.

   The socket-outlet shown in the bedroom with the shower cubicle must be outside zone 3.

Diagram 1(b) Illustration of earthing and bonding conductors that might be part of the electrical installation shown in Diagram 1(a)

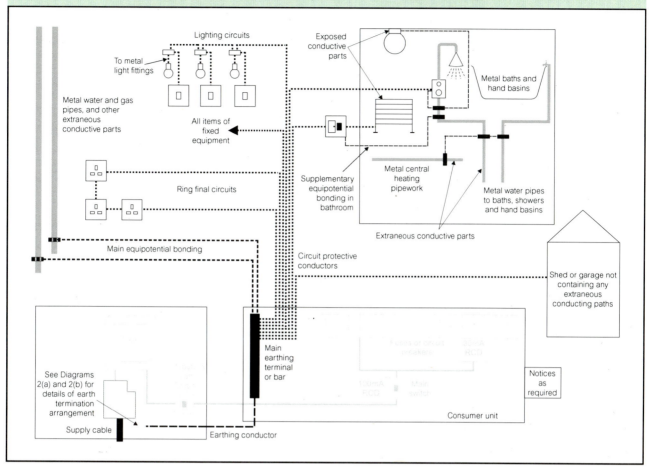

Notes:

1. See the general rules in BS 7671:2001.

2. Circuit protective conductors are taken to all items of fixed electrical equipment and local isolation and switching devices which appear in Diagram 1(a).

3. In the case of a protective multiple earthing (PME) supply (see Diagram 2(a)), consult the electricity distributor.

4. Supplementary bonding is required in bathrooms to an extent dependent upon the presence of metallic fixtures, fittings and pipework: see Section 601 of BS 7671:2001.

Diagram 2(a) **Example earthing arrangement where the electricity distributor provides the earth connection (referred to as TN-C-S where the connection is made to A, or TN-S where the connection is made to B – the most common systems in urban areas)**

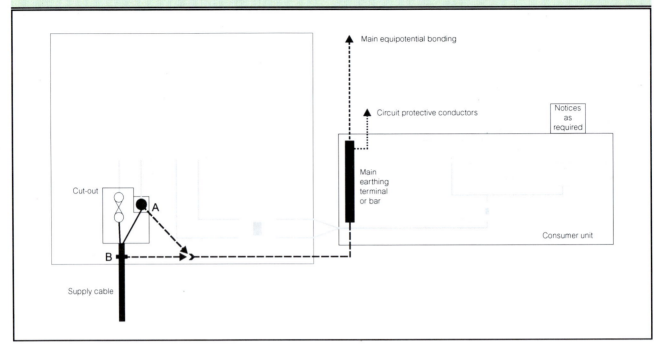

Notes:

1. Connection A shows the arrangement where an electricity distributor provides a combined protective earthing and neutral conductor as part of a protective multiple earthing system (referred to as TN-C-S).

    Connection B shows the arrangement where an electricity distributor provides a protective earthing conductor (usually the metallic covering of the supply cable) that is separate from the neutral conductor (as part of a system referred to as TN-S).

2. Connection A or B can only be made by the electricity distributor or its appointed agent.

Diagram 2(b) Example earthing arrangement where consumers provide their own earthing connection (referred to as a TT system)

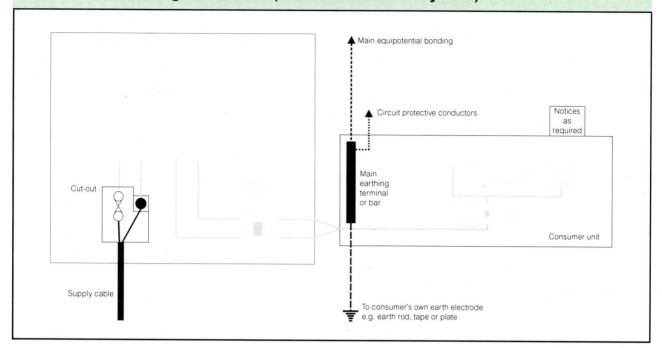

Notes:

1. BS 7671:2001 requires that the part of the installation between the origin and the first RCD shall comply with the requirements for protection by Class II equipment or equivalent insulation. For the arrangement shown, this applies to the consumer unit and the wiring connecting it to the supplier's equipment.

2. The 100mA RCD component of the main switch should be of the time delayed type.

Appendix B: Copies of BS 7671 and IEE model forms

The BS 7671 and IEE forms and notes on the following pages are taken from IEE Guidance Note 3, 2002 edition, and are available for downloading from the IEE website at www.iee.org/Publish/WireRegs/forms.cfm.

They appear in the order:

Introduction

1. Introduction to Appendix 6 of BS 7671:2001 (Model forms for certification and reporting).

Initial inspection and testing

2. Notes for short form and full versions of Electrical Installation Certificate.

3. Form 1 – Short form of Electrical Installation Certificate (for use when one person is responsible for the design, construction, inspection and testing of an installation), including guidance for recipients.

4. Form 2 – Full Electrical Installation Certificate, including guidance for recipients (standard form from Appendix 6 of BS 7671).

5. Form 3 – Schedule of Inspections (from Appendix 6 of BS 7671) with notes.

6. Form 4 – Schedule of Test Results (from Appendix 6 of BS 7671) with notes.

Minor works

7. Notes on completion of Minor Electrical Installation Works Certificate.

8. Form 5 – Minor Electrical Installation Works Certificate, including guidance for recipients (from Appendix 6 of BS 7671).

CERTIFICATION AND REPORTING

Introduction

i. The Electrical Installation Certificate required by Part 7 of BS 7671 shall be made out and signed or otherwise authenticated by a competent person or persons in respect of the design, construction, inspection and testing of the work.

ii. The Minor Works Certificate required by Part 7 of BS 7671 shall be made out and signed or otherwise authenticated by a competent person in respect of the inspection and testing of an installation.

iii. The Periodic Inspection Report required by Part 7 of BS 7671 shall be made out and signed or otherwise authenticated by a competent person in respect of the inspection and testing of an installation.

iv. Competent persons will, as appropriate to their function under (i) (ii) and (iii) above, have a sound knowledge and experience relevant to the nature of the work undertaken and to the technical standards set down in this British Standard, be fully versed in the inspection and testing procedures contained in this Standard and employ adequate testing equipment.

v. Electrical Installation Certificates will indicate the responsibility for design, construction, inspection and testing, whether in relation to new work or further work on an existing installation.

Where design, construction and inspection and testing are the responsibility of one person, a Certificate with a single signature declaration in the form shown below may replace the multiple signatures section of the model form.

FOR DESIGN, CONSTRUCTION, INSPECTION & TESTING.

I being the person responsible for the Design, Construction, Inspection & Testing of the electrical installation (as indicated by my signature below), particulars of which are described above, having exercised reasonable skill and care when carrying out the Design, Construction, Inspection & Testing, hereby CERTIFY that the said work for which I have been responsible is to the best of my knowledge and belief in accordance with BS 7671: ...., amended to .... (date) except for the departures, if any, detailed as follows.

vi. A Minor Works Certificate will indicate the responsibility for design, construction, inspection and testing of the work described in Part 4 of the certificate.

vii. A Periodic Inspection Report will indicate the responsibility for the inspection and testing of an installation within the extent and limitations specified on the report.

viii. A schedule of inspections and a schedule of test results as required by Part 7 (of BS 7671) shall be issued with the associated Electrical Installation Certificate or Periodic Inspection Report.

ix. When making out and signing a form on behalf of a company or other business entity, individuals shall state for whom they are acting.

x. Additional forms may be required as clarification, if needed by non-technical persons, or in expansion, for larger or more complex installations.

xi. The IEE Guidance Note 3 provides further information on inspection and testing on completion and for periodic inspections.

Electrical installation certificates
Notes for Forms 1 and 2

1. The Electrical Installation Certificate is to be used only for the initial certification of a new installation or for an alteration or addition to an existing installation where new circuits have been introduced.

    It is not to be used for a Periodic Inspection for which a Periodic Inspection Report form should be used. For an alteration or addition which does not extend to the introduction of new circuits, a Minor Electrical Installation Works Certificate may be used.

    The original Certificate is to be given to the person ordering the work (Regulation 742-01-03). A duplicate should be retained by the contractor.

2. This Certificate is only valid if accompanied by the Schedule of Inspections and the Schedule(s) of Test Results.

3. The signatures appended are those of the persons authorised by the companies executing the work of design, construction and inspection and testing respectively. A signatory authorised to certify more than one category of work should sign in each of the appropriate places.

4. The time interval recommended before the first periodic inspection must be inserted (see IEE Guidance Note 3 for guidance).

5. The page numbers for each of the Schedules of Test Results should be indicated, together with the total number of sheets involved.

6. The maximum prospective fault current recorded should be the greater of either the short-circuit current or the earth fault current.

7. The proposed date for the next inspection should take into consideration the frequency and quality of maintenance that the installation can reasonably be expected to receive during its intended life, and the period should be agreed between the designer, installer and other relevant parties.

Form 1　　　　　　　　　　　　　　　　　　　　　　　　　　　　　Form No.　　　/1

ELECTRICAL INSTALLATION CERTIFICATE (notes 1 and 2)

(REQUIREMENTS FOR ELECTRICAL INSTALLATIONS – BS 7671 (IEE WIRING REGULATIONS))

DETAILS OF THE CLIENT (note 1)

....

....

....

INSTALLATION ADDRESS

....

....

.... Postcode ....

DESCRIPTION AND EXTENT OF THE INSTALLATION Tick boxes as appropriate

Description of installation: ....

Extent of installation covered by this Certificate: ....

....

....

....

....

New installation	☐
Addition to an existing installation	☐
Alteration to an existing installation	☐

FOR DESIGN, CONSTRUCTION, INSPECTION & TESTING

I being the person responsible for the Design, Construction, Inspection & Testing of the electrical installation (as indicated by my signature below), particulars of which are described above, having exercised reasonable skill and care when carrying out the Design, Construction, Inspection & Testing, hereby CERTIFY that the said work for which I have been responsible is to the best of my knowledge and belief in accordance with BS 7671 : ...., amended to .... (date) except for the departures, if any, detailed as follows:

> Details of departures from BS 7671 (Regulations 120-01-03, 120-02):

The extent of liability of the signatory is limited to the work described above as the subject of this Certificate.

Name (IN BLOCK LETTERS): ....　　Position: ....

Signature (note 3): ....　　Date: ....

For and on behalf of: ....

Address: ....

....

.... Postcode...........................　　Tel No: ....

NEXT INSPECTION

I recommend that this installation is further inspected and tested after an interval of not more than .... years/months (notes 4 and 7)

SUPPLY CHARACTERISTICS AND EARTHING ARRANGEMENTS Tick boxes and enter details, as appropriate

Earthing arrangements	Number and Type of Live Conductors		Nature of Supply Parameters	Supply Protective Device Characteristics
TN-C ☐	a.c. ☐	d.c. ☐	Nominal voltage, $U/U_o^{(1)}$ V	
TN-S ☐	1-phase, 2-wire ☐	2-pole ☐	Nominal frequency, $f^{(1)}$ ....Hz	Type:.......................
TN-C-S ☐	1-phase, 3-wire ☐	3-pole ☐	Prospective fault current, Ipf $^{(2)}$ (note 6)........kA	....
TT ☐	2-phase, 3 wire ☐	other ☐	External loop impedance, Ze$^{(2)}$ ....Ω	
IT ☐	3-phase, 3-wire ☐		(Note: (1) by enquiry, (2) by enquiry or by measurement)	Nominal current rating
☐	3-phase, 4-wire ☐			.................................A
Alternative source ☐ of supply (to be detailed on attached schedules)				

PARTICULARS OF INSTALLATION REFERRED TO IN THE CERTIFICATE Tick boxes and enter details, as appropriate

Means of Earthing

Distributor's facility ☐

Installation earth electrode ☐

Maximum Demand

Maximum demand (load).. Amps per phase

Details of Installation Earth Electrode (where applicable)

Type (e.g. rod(s), tape, etc.)	Location	Electrode resistance to earth
....	....	.....................................Ω

Main Protective Conductors

Earthing conductor: material ....   csa ....mm²   connection verified ☐

Main equipotential bonding conductors   material ....   csa ....mm²   connection verified ☐

To incoming water and/or gas service ☐   To other elements...

Main Switch or Circuit-breaker

BS, Type ....   No. of poles ....   Current rating ....A   Voltage rating V

Location ....   Fuse rating or setting......................A

Rated residual operating current I $_{\Delta n}$ = ... mA, and operating time of .... ms (at I $_{\Delta n}$)

(applicable only where an RCD is suitable and is used as a main circuit-breaker)

COMMENTS ON EXISTING INSTALLATION: (In the case of an alteration or additions see Section 743)

....
....
....
....
....
....
....
....
....

SCHEDULES (note 2)

The attached Schedules are part of this document and this Certificate is valid only when they are attached to it.

.... Schedules of Inspections and .... Schedules of Test Results are attached.

(Enter quantities of schedules attached)

GUIDANCE FOR RECIPIENTS

This safety Certificate has been issued to confirm that the electrical installation work to which it relates has been designed, constructed and inspected and tested in accordance with British Standard 7671 (The IEE Wiring Regulations).

You should have received an original Certificate and the contractor should have retained a duplicate Certificate. If you were the person ordering the work, but not the user of the installation, you should pass this Certificate, or a full copy of it including the schedules, immediately to the user.

The 'original' Certificate should be retained in a safe place and be shown to any person inspecting or undertaking further work on the electrical installation in the future. If you later vacate the property, this Certificate will demonstrate to the new owner that the electrical installation complied with the requirements of British Standard 7671 at the time the Certificate was issued. The Construction (Design and Management) Regulations require that for a project covered by those Regulations, a copy of this Certificate, together with schedules, is included in the project health and safety documentation.

For safety reasons, the electrical installation will need to be inspected at appropriate intervals by a competent person. The maximum time interval recommended before the next inspection is stated on Page 1 under 'Next Inspection'.

This Certificate is intended to be issued only for a new electrical installation or for new work associated with an alteration or addition to an existing installation. It should not have been issued for the inspection of an existing electrical installation. A 'Periodic Inspection Report' should be issued for such a periodic inspection.

Form 2
Form No. /2

ELECTRICAL INSTALLATION CERTIFICATE (notes 1 and 2)

(REQUIREMENTS FOR ELECTRICAL INSTALLATIONS – BS 7671 (IEE WIRING REGULATIONS))

DETAILS OF THE CLIENT (note 1) ....

INSTALLATION ADDRESS

.... Postcode ....

DESCRIPTION AND EXTENT OF THE INSTALLATION Tick boxes as appropriate

(note 1)

Description of installation: ....

Extent of installation covered by this Certificate: ....

New installation	☐
Addition to an existing installation	☐
Alteration to an existing installation	☐

FOR DESIGN

I/We being the person(s) responsible for the design of the electrical installation (as indicated by my/our signatures below), particulars of which are described above, having exercised reasonable skill and care when carrying out the design, hereby CERTIFY that the design work for which I/we have been responsible is to the best of my/our knowledge and belief in accordance with BS 7671 : ...., amended to .... (date) except for the departures, if any, detailed as follows:

> Details of departures from BS 7671 (Regulations 120-01-03, 120-02):

The extent of liability of the signatory or the signatories is limited to the work described above as the subject of this Cerificate.

For the DESIGN of the installation: **(Where there is mutual responsibility for the design)

Signature: .... Date .... Name (BLOCK LETTERS): ....Designer No. 1

Signature: .... Date .... Name (BLOCK LETTERS): ....Designer No. 2**

FOR CONSTRUCTION

I/We being the person(s) responsible for the construction of the electrical installation (as indicated by my/our signatures below), particulars of which are described above, having exercised reasonable skill and care when carrying out the construction, hereby CERTIFY that the construction work for which I/we have been responsible is to the best of my/our knowledge and belief in accordance with BS 7671: ...., amended to .... (date) except for the departures, if any, detailed as follows:

> Details of departures from BS 7671 (Regulations 120-01-03, 120-02):

The extent of liability of the signatory is limited to the work described above as the subject of this Certificate.

For CONSTRUCTION of the installation:

Signature: .... Date ....

Name (BLOCK LETTERS) .... Constructor

FOR INSPECTION & TESTING

I/We being the person(s) responsible for the inspection & testing of the electrical installation (as indicated by my/our signatures below), particulars of which are described above, having exercised reasonable skill and care when carrying out the inspection & testing, hereby CERTIFY that the work for which I/we have been responsible is to the best of my knowledge and belief in accordance with BS 7671: ...., amended to .... (date) except for the departures, if any, detailed as follows:

> Details of departures from BS 7671 (Regulations 120-01-03, 120-02):

The extent of liability of the signatory is limited to the work described above as the subject of this Certificate.

For INSPECTION & TEST of the installation:

Signature: .... Date ....

Name (BLOCK LETTERS) .... Inspector

NEXT INSPECTION (notes 4 and 7)

I/We the designer(s) recommend that this installation is further inspected and tested after an interval of not more than .... years/months

PARTICULARS OF THE SIGNATORIES TO THE ELECTRICAL INSTALLATION CERTIFICATE (note 3)

Designer (No 1)

Name: .... Company: ....

Address: ....

.... Postcode: .... Tel No: ....

Designer (No 2)
(if applicable)

Name: .... Company: ....

Address: ....

.... Postcode: .... Tel No: ....

Constructor

Name: .... Company: ....

Address: ....

.... Postcode: .... Tel No: ....

Inspector

Name: .... Company: ....

Address: ....

.... Postcode: .... Tel No: ....

SUPPLY CHARACTERISTICS AND EARTHING ARRANGEMENTS Tick boxes and enter details, as appropriate

Earthing arrangements	Number of Type of Live Conductors		Nature of Supply Parameters	Supply Protective Device Characteristics
TN-C ☐	a.c. ☐	d.c. ☐	Nominal voltage, U/Uo$^{(1)}$ V	
TN-S ☐	1-phase, 2-wire ☐	2-pole ☐	Nominal frequency, f$^{(1)}$ ....Hz	Type:..........................
TN-C-S ☐	1-phase, 3-wire ☐	3-pole ☐	Prospective fault current, Ipf$^{(2)}$ (note 6)........kA	....
TT ☐	2-phase, 3 wire ☐	other ☐	External loop impedance, Ze$^{(2)}$ ....Ω	
IT ☐	3-phase, 3-wire ☐		(Note: (1) by enquiry. (2) by enquiry or by measurement)	Nominal current rating
☐	3-phase, 4-wire ☐			................................A
Alternative source ☐ of supply (to be detailed on attached schedules)				

PARTICULARS OF INSTALLATION REFERRED TO IN THE CERTIFICATE Tick boxes and enter details, as appropriate

Means of Earthing

Distributor's facility ☐

Installation earth electrode ☐

Maximum Demand

Maximum demand (load).. Amps per phase

Details of Installation Earth Electrode (where applicable)

Type (e.g. rod(s), tape, etc.)	Location	Electrode resistance to earth
....	....	...................................Ω

Main Protective Conductors

Earthing conductor: material ....   csa ....mm^2 connection verified ☐

Main equipotential bonding conductors   material ....   csa ....mm^2 connection verified ☐

To incoming water and/or gas service ☐   To other elements...

Main Switch or Circuit-breaker

BS. Type ....   No. of poles ....   Current rating ....A   Voltage rating V

Location ....   Fuse rating or setting.......................A

Rated residual operating current I $_{\Delta n}$ = ... mA, and operating time of .... ms (at I $_{\Delta n}$)

(applicable only where an RCD is suitable and is used as a main circuit-breaker)

COMMENTS ON EXISTING INSTALLATION: (In the case of an alteration or additions see Section 743)

....

....

....

....

SCHEDULES (note 2)

The attached Schedules are part of this document and this Certificate is valid only when they are attached to it.

.... Schedules of Inspections and .... Schedules of Test Results are attached. (Enter quantities of schedules attached)

ELECTRICAL INSTALLATION CERTIFICATE
GUIDANCE FOR RECIPIENTS (to be appended to the Certificate)

This safety Certificate has been issued to confirm that the electrical installation work to which it relates has been designed, constructed and inspected and tested in accordance with British Standard 7671 (The IEE Wiring Regulations).

You should have received an original Certificate and the contractor should have retained a duplicate Certificate. If you were the person ordering the work, but not the user of the installation, you should pass this Certificate, or a full copy of it including the schedules, immediately to the user.

The 'original' Certificate should be retained in a safe place and be shown to any person inspecting or undertaking further work on the electrical installation in the future. If you later vacate the property, this Certificate will demonstrate to the new owner that the electrical installation complied with the requirements of British Standard 7671 at the time the Certificate was issued. The Construction (Design and Management) Regulations require that for a project covered by those Regulations, a copy of this Certificate, together with schedules, is included in the project health and safety documentation.

For safety reasons, the electrical installation will need to be inspected at appropriate intervals by a competent person. The maximum time interval recommended before the next inspection is stated on Page 1 under 'Next Inspection'.

This Certificate is intended to be issued only for a new electrical installation or for new work associated with an alteration or addition to an existing installation. It should not have been issued for the inspection of an existing electrical installation. A 'Periodic Inspection Report' should be issued for such a periodic inspection.

The Certificate is only valid if a Schedule of Inspections and Schedule of Test Result are appended.

Form 3   Form No.   /3
SCHEDULE OF INSPECTIONS

Methods of protection against electric shock

(a)   Protection against both direct and indirect contact:

☐   (i)   SELV (note 1)

☐   (ii)   Limitation of discharge of energy

(b)   Protection against direct contact: (note 2)

☐   (i)   Insulation of live parts

☐   (ii)   Barriers or enclosures

☐   (iii)   Obstacles (note 3)

☐   (iv)   Placing out of reach (note 4)

☐   (v)   PELV

☐   (vi)   Presence of RCD for supplementary protection

(c)   Protection against indirect contact:

(i)   EEBADS including:

☐   Presence of earthing conductor

☐   Presence of circuit protective conductors

☐   Presence of main equipotential bonding conductors

☐   Presence of supplementary equipotential bonding conductors

☐   Presence of earthing arrangements for combined protective and functional purposes

☐   Presence of adequate arrangements for alternative source(s), where applicable

☐   Presence of residual current device(s)

☐   (ii)   Use of Class II equipment or equivalent insulation (note 5)

☐   (iii)   Non-conducting location: (note 6) Absence of protective conductors

☐   (iv)   Earth-free equipotential bonding: (note 7) Presence of earth-free equipotential bonding conductors

☐   (v)   Electrical separation (note 8)

Prevention of mutual detrimental influence

☐   (a)   Proximity of non-electrical services and other influences

☐   (b)   Segregation of band I and band II circuits or band II insulation used

☐   (c)   Segregation of safety circuits

Identification

☐   (a)   Presence of diagrams, instructions, circuit charts and similar information

☐   (b)   Presence of danger notices and other warning notices

☐   (c)   Labelling of protective devices, switches and terminals

☐   (d)   Identification of conductors

Cables and conductors

☐   (a)   Routing of cables in prescribed zones or within mechanical protection

☐   (b)   Connection of conductors

☐   (c)   Erection methods

☐   (d)   Selection of conductors for current-carrying capacity and voltage drop

☐   (e)   Presence of fire barriers, suitable seals and protection against thermal effects

General

☐   (a)   Presence and correct location of appropriate devices for isolation and switching

☐   (b)   Adquacy of access to switchgear and other equipment

☐   (c)   Particular protective measures for special installations and locations

☐   (d)   Connection of single-pole devices for protection or switching in phase conductors only

☐   (e)   Correct connection of accessories and equipment

☐   (f)   Presence of undervoltage protective devices

☐   (g)   Choice and setting of protective and monitoring devices for protection against indirect contact and/or overcurrent

☐   (h)   Selection of equipment and protective measures appropriate to external influences

☐   (i)   Selection of appropriate functional switching devices

Inspected by ....   Date ....

Notes:

T   to indicate an inspection has been carried out and the result is satisfactory

C   to indicate an inspection has been carried out and the result was unsatisfactory

N/A   to indicate the inspection is not applicable

LIM   to indicate that, exceptionally, a limitation agreed with the person ordering the work prevented the inspection or test being carried out

1.   SELV – an extra-low voltage system which is electrically separated from earth and from other systems. The particular requirements of the Regulations must be checked (see Regulations 411-02 and 471-02)

2.   Method of protection against direct contact – will include measurement of distances where appropriate

3.   Obstacles – only adopted in special circumstances (see Regulations 412-04 and 471-06)

4.   Placing out of reach – only adopted in special circumstances (see Regulations 412-05 and 471-07)

5.   Use of Class II equipment – infrequently adopted and only when the installation is to be supervised (see Regulations 413-03 and 471-09)

6.   Non-conducting locations – not applicable in domestic premises and requiring special precautions (see Regulations 413-04 and 471-10)

7.   Earth-free local equipotential bonding – not applicable in domestic premises, only used in special circumstances (see Regulations 413-05 and 471-11)

8.   Electrical separation (see Regulations 413-06 and 471-12)

Form 4

Form No ..../4

SCHEDULE OF TEST RESULTS

Contractor: ....

Test Date: ....

Signature: ....

Address/Location of distribution board: ....

* Type of Supply: TN-S/TN-C-S/TT
* Ze at origin: ....ohms
* PFC: ....kA

Instruments
loop impedance: ....
continuity: ....
insulation: ....
RCD tester: ....

Method of protection against indirect contact: ....

Equipment vulnerable to testing: ....

Description of Work:

Circuit Description	Overcurrent Device			Wiring Conductors		Continuity			Insulation Resistance		Polarity	Earth Loop Impedance	Functional Testing		Remarks
	*Short-circuit capacity: ....kA														
	type	Rating I_n A	live mm²	cpc mm²	(R₁ + R₂)* Ω	R₂* Ω	Ring	Live/ Live Ω	Live/ Earth MΩ		Zs Ω	RCD time ms	Other	
1	2	3	4	5	*6	7	*8	*9	*10	*11	*12	*13	*14	15

Test Results

Deviations from Wiring Regulations and special notes:

* See notes on schedule of test results

Notes on schedule of test results

* **Type of supply** is ascertained from the supply company or by inspection.

* **Ze at origin.** When the maximum value declared by the electricity supplier is used, the effectiveness of the earth must be confirmed by a test. If measured the main bonding will need to be disconnected for the duration of the test.

* **Short-circuit capacity** of the device is noted, see Table 7.2A of the On-Site Guide or 2.7.15 of GN3.

* **Prospective fault current (PFC).** The value recorded is the greater of either the short-circuit current or the earth fault current. Preferably determined by enquiry of the supplier.

The following tests, where relevant, shall be carried out in the following sequence:

Continuity of protective conductors, including main and supplementary bonding

Every protective conductor, including main and supplementary bonding conductors, should be tested to verify that it is continuous and correctly connected.

*6   Continuity

Where Test Method 1 is used, enter the measured resistance of the phase conductor plus the circuit protective conductor (R1+ R2).

See 10.3.1 of the On-Site Guide or 2.7.5 of GN3.

During the continuity testing (Test Method 1) the following polarity checks are to be carried out:

a. every fuse and single-pole control and protective device is connected in the phase conductor only;

b. centre-contact bayonet and Edison screw lampholders have outer contact connected to the neutral conductor;

c. wiring is correctly connected to socket-outlets and similar accessories.

Compliance is to be indicated by a tick in polarity column 11.

(R1 + R2) need not be recorded if R2 is recorded in column 7.

*7

Where Test Method 2 is used, the maximum value of R2 is recorded in column 7.

Where the alternative method of Regulation 413-02-12 is used for shock protection, the resistance of the circuit protective conductor R2 is measured and recorded in column 7.

See 10.3.1 of the On-Site Guide or 2.7.5 of GN3.

*8   Continuity of ring final circuit conductors

A test shall be made to verify the continuity of each conductor including the protective conductor of every ring final circuit.

See 10.3.2 of the On-Site Guide or 2.7.6 of GN3.

*9,*10   Insulation resistance

All voltage sensitive devices to be disconnected or test between live conductors (phase and neutral) connected together and earth.

The insulation resistance between live conductors is to be inserted in column 9.

The minimum insulation resistance values are given in Table 10.1 of the On-Site Guide or Table 2.2 of GN3.

See 10.3.3(iv) of the On-Site Guide or 2.7.7 of GN3.

All the preceding tests should be carried out before the installation is energised.

*11   Polarity

A satisfactory polarity test may be indicated by a tick in column 11.

Only in a Schedule of Test Results associated with a Periodic Inspection Report is it acceptable to record incorrect polarity.

*12   **Earth fault loop impedance Zs**

This may be determined either by direct measurement at the furthest point of a live circuit or by adding (R1 + R2) of column 6 to Ze. Ze is determined by measurement at the origin of the installation or preferably the value declared by the supply company used.

$Zs = Ze + (R1 + R2)$. Zs should be less than the values given in Appendix 2 of the On-Site Guide or Appendix 2 of GN3.

*13   **Functional testing**

The operation of RCDs (including RCBOs) shall be tested by simulating a fault condition, independent of any test facility in the device.

Record operating time in column 13. Effectiveness of the test button must be confirmed.

See Section 11 of the On-Site Guide or 2.7.16 of GN3.

*14   All switchgear and controlgear assemblies, drives, control and interlocks, etc. must be operated to ensure that they are properly mounted, adjusted and installed.

Satisfactory operation is indicated by a tick in column 14.

Earth electrode resistance

The earth electrode resistance of TT installations must be measured, and normally an RCD is required.

For reliability in service the resistance of any earth electrode should be below 200Ω. Record the value on Form 1, 2 or 6, as appropriate.

See 10.3.5 of the On-Site Guide or 2.7.13 of GN3.

Form 5

MINOR ELECTRICAL INSTALLATION WORKS CERTIFICATE

(REQUIREMENTS FOR ELECTRICAL INSTALLATIONS – BS 7671 (IEE WIRING REGULATIONS))

To be used only for minor electrical work which does not include the provision of a new circuit

---

PART 1 : Description of minor works

1. Description of the minor works:..

2. Location/Address: ....

3. Date minor works completed:...

4. Details of departures, if any, from BS 7671

   ....

   ....

   ....

PART 2 : Installation details

1. System earthing arrangement: TN-C-S ☐   TN-S ☐   TT ☐

2. Method of protection against indirect contact: ....

3. Protective device for the modified circuit: Type BS ....   Rating ....A

4. Comments on existing installation, including adequacy of earthing and bonding arrangements:
   (See Regulation 130-07) ....

   ....

   ....

   ....

PART 3 : Essential Tests

1. Earthing continuity: satisfactory ☐

2. Insulation resistance:

   Phase/neutral...$M\Omega$

   Phase/earth ....$M\Omega$

   Neutral/earth..$M\Omega$

3. Earth fault loop impedance   ....Ω

4. Polarity: satisfactory   ☐

5. RCD operation (if applicable): Rated residual operating current $I_{\Delta n}$..........mA and operating time of ....ms (at $I_{\Delta n}$)

PART 4 : Declaration

1. I/We CERTIFY that the said works do not impair the safety of the existing installation, that the said works have been designed, constructed, inspected and tested in accordance with BS 7671 : .... (IEE Wiring Regulations), amended to .... and that the said works, to the best of my/our knowledge and belief, at the time of my/our inspection, complied with BS 7671 except as detailed in Part 1.

2. Name: ....   3. Signature:...

   For and on behalf of: ....   Position:..

   Address: ....

   ....   Date: ....

   ....

   ....Postcode ....

MINOR ELECTRICAL INSTALLATION WORKS CERTIFICATE
GUIDANCE FOR RECIPIENTS (to be appended to the Certificate)

This Certificate has been issued to confirm that the electrical installation work to which it relates has been designed, constructed and inspected and tested in accordance with British Standard 7671 (The IEE Wiring Regulations).

You should have received an original Certificate and the contractor should have retained a duplicate. If you were the person ordering the work, but not the owner of the installation, you should pass this Certificate, or a copy of it, to the owner.

A separate Certificate should have been received for each existing circuit on which minor works have been carried out. This Certificate is not appropriate if you requested the contractor to undertake more extensive installation work, for which you should have received an Electrical Installation Certificate.

The Certificate should be retained in a safe place and be shown to any person inspecting or undertaking further work on the electrical installation in the future. If you later vacate the property, this Certificate will demonstrate to the new owner that the minor electrical installation work carried out complied with the requirements of British Standard 7671 at the time the Certificate was issued.

Notes on completion of minor electrical installation works certificate

Scope

The Minor Works Certificate is intended to be used for additions and alterations to an installation that do not extend to the provision of a new circuit. Examples include the addition of a socket-outlet or a lighting point to an existing circuit, the relocation of a light switch, etc. This Certificate may also be used for the replacement of equipment such as accessories or luminaires, but not for the replacement of distribution boards or similar items. Appropriate inspection and testing, however, should always be carried out irrespective of the extent of the work undertaken.

Part 1 Description of minor works

1, 2   The minor works must be so described that the work that is the subject of the certification can be readily identified.

4   See Regulations 120-01-03 and 120-02. No departures are to be expected except in most unusual circumstances. See also Regulation 743-01-01.

Part 2 Installation details

2   The method of protection against indirect contact shock must be clearly identified, e.g. earthed equipotential bonding and automatic disconnection of supply using fuse/circuit-breaker/RCD.

4   If the existing installation lacks either an effective means of earthing or adequate main equipotential bonding conductors, this must be clearly stated. See Regulation 743-01-02.

Recorded departures from BS 7671 may constitute non-compliance with the Electricity Supply Regulations 1988 as amended or the Electricity at Work Regulations 1989. It is important that the client is advised immediately in writing.

Part 3 Essential tests

The relevant provisions of Part 7 (Inspection and Testing) of BS 7671 must be applied in full to all minor works. For example, where a socket-outlet is added to an existing circuit it is necessary to:

1   establish that the earthing contact of the socket-outlet is connected to the main earthing terminal;

2   measure the insulation resistance of the circuit that has been added to, and establish that it complies with Table 71A of BS 7671;

3   measure the earth fault loop impedance to establish that the maximum permitted disconnection time is not exceeded;

4   check that the polarity of the socket-outlet is correct;

5   (if the work is protected by an RCD) verify the effectiveness of the RCD.

Part 4 Declaration

1, 3   The Certificate shall be made out and signed by a competent person in respect of the design, construction, inspection and testing of the work.

1, 3   The competent person will have a sound knowledge and experience relevant to the nature of the work undertaken and to the technical standards set down in BS 7671, be fully versed in the inspection and testing procedures contained in the Regulations and employ adequate testing equipment.

2   When making out and signing a form on behalf of a company or other business entity, individuals shall state for whom they are acting.

Appendix C: Older practice that can be encountered in alteration work

When carrying out work on existing, older installations, some features will be encountered which differ from those found in modern installations.

Electrical installations began to be commonplace in domestic dwellings as early as the 1920s, and over the years there have been considerable changes to the types of wiring materials and other equipment being installed, and in the ways that electrical installations are structured. From the electrical safety point of view, these changes have had two main causes: advances in technology, and amendments to the Wiring Regulations published by the Institution of Electrical Engineers (issued as British Standard BS 7671 since 1992).

This appendix presents examples of the types of features just mentioned, which may be unfamiliar to those who find them and may be a safety hazard. Also included, where applicable, are comments about changes in the Wiring Regulations relevant to the equipment concerned.

Use of a gas, water or other service pipe as an earth

(No proper means of earthing for the electrical installation)

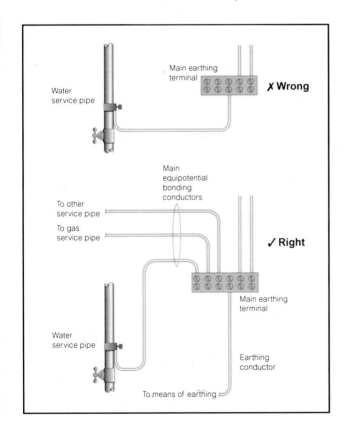

It is not permitted to use a gas, water or other metal service pipe as a means of earthing for an electrical installation. (This does not preclude equipotential bonding connections to these pipes.) It never has been permitted for gas pipes, and has not been permitted for other service pipes since 1966.

Every electrical installation requires a proper means of earthing. The most usual type is an electricity distributor's earthing terminal, provided for this purpose near the electricity meter.

Absence of, or inadequately sized, main equipotential bonding conductors

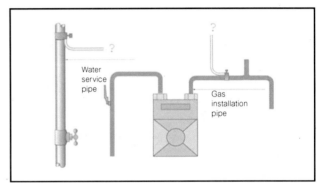

Prior to 1966 the Wiring Regulations contained no requirements for main equipotential bonding.

Since then, the installation of main equipotential bonding conductors has been required to water service pipes, gas installation pipes, oil supply pipes and certain other 'earthy' metalwork that may be present on the premises.

During the 1980s new Regulations were introduced, requiring the minimum size of main equipotential bonding conductors to be larger than previously called for, particularly where there is a PME (protective multiple earthing) electricity supply. For most dwellings the minimum size now permitted to be installed is 10mm^2.

Absence of, or inadequately sized, supplementary equipotential bonding

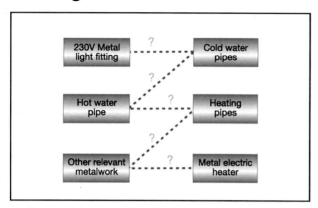

Prior to 1981 there were virtually no requirements in the Wiring Regulations for supplementary equipotential bonding conductors.

Since then, the installation of supplementary equipotential bonding conductors has been required in installations and locations of increased electric shock risk, such as bathrooms and shower rooms.

During the 1980s and 1990s the requirements for the sizing of supplementary equipotential bonding conductors were amended. For most dwellings the minimum size now permitted to be installed without mechanical protection is 4mm².

Double-pole fusing

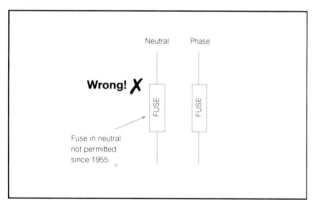

In many installations put in up to the 1950s, the circuits have a fuse in the neutral conductor as well as in the phase conductor. This is a potentially dangerous practice for ac installations, and ceased to be permitted by the Wiring Regulations in about 1955.

In the event of a short circuit, there is a 50% chance that the fuse in the neutral conductor will operate. When this happens, the phase conductor is not automatically disconnected from the faulty circuit as would now normally be expected, thereby leaving a danger for the unwary.

Voltage-operated earth-leakage circuit-breakers

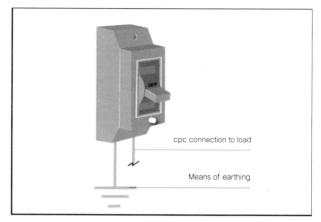

Two basic types of earth-leakage circuit-breaker used to be recognised by the Wiring Regulations: the current-operated type and the voltage-operated type. Today, only the current-operated type is recognised (now called residual current devices or RCDs).

The voltage-operated type ceased to be recognised in 1981. It can be distinguished by its two separate earthing terminals – one for an earthing connection to the load and one for an earthing connection to a means of earthing (often a driven rod). The major drawback with this type of device is that a parallel earth path can render it disabled.

No circuit protective conductors in lighting circuits

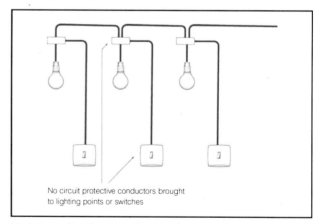

Lighting circuits installed before 1966, and not including any metalwork needing to be earthed, often do not include a circuit protective conductor. Consequently, any new or replacement light fittings, switches or other components must be of a type not requiring earthing, e.g. non-metallic varieties, unless new circuit protective (earthing) conductors are provided. Otherwise, there will be a potential danger of indirect contact (electric shock).

All lighting circuits installed since 1966 (with the exception of certain extra-low voltage circuits) have been required to include a circuit protective conductor.

Non-13A socket-outlets

The installation of socket-outlets other than the current standard 13A square-pinned type was common prior to the early 1950s. These outlets accept non-fused plugs (some with an earth pin and some without), generally having round pins.

These older types of socket-outlet designed for non-fused plugs must not be connected to a ring circuit. Such an arrangement can be dangerous.

In addition, socket-outlets that will accept unearthed (2-pin) plugs must not be used to supply equipment needing to be earthed. It is strongly recommended that such outlets be taken out of service.

No RCD protection for socket-outlets likely to supply portable equipment outdoors

(or insufficient number of such socket-outlets so protected)

A person receiving an electric shock when using portable electrical equipment outdoors can be at great risk of death or serious injury. The risk is significantly reduced if the socket-outlet supplying the equipment is provided with sensitive RCD protection (fitted either at the socket-outlet itself or at the consumer unit). However, prior to 1981 the Wiring Regulations did not require such protection.

Nowadays, sensitive RCD protection[6] is required for all socket-outlets which are installed having a rating of 32A or less, and which may reasonably be expected to supply portable equipment for use outdoors. The initial requirement, in 1981, was for this protection to be provided to at least one such socket-outlet. However, this was found to be inadequate.

Green coloured protective conductors or sleeving instead of green–yellow

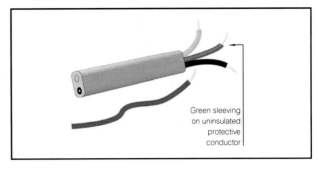

Green sleeving on uninsulated protective conductor

The Wiring Regulations used to accept the single colour green for the identification of protective conductors.

However, since 1977 a green–yellow coding has been required for all protective conductors installed.

The older green sleeving or tape should be replaced with the new green–yellow striped variety whenever connections are re-made.

Concealed cables outside of permitted zones in walls

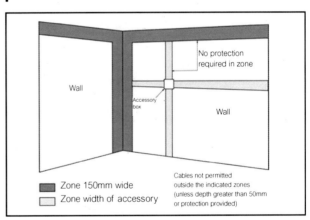

No protection required in zone

Wall

Accessory box

Wall

Zone 150mm wide
Zone width of accessory

Cables not permitted outside the indicated zones (unless depth greater than 50mm or protection provided)

Until the latter part of the 1980s the Wiring Regulations did not contain any specific requirements for the positioning of cables concealed in walls and partitions.

Today's requirements are given in Regulation 522-06-06 in BS 7671, and are illustrated here.

To avoid striking a cable, extreme care should always be taken in any activity that involves penetrating a wall or partition, even when it is known that any concealed cables were installed in recent years. Where the cables were installed prior to 1980 they are particularly likely to be found outside of the zones illustrated opposite. A cable and stud detector should always be used before attempting to drill into walls, floors or ceilings.

---

6   The RCD should have a rated residual operating current of not more than 30mA.

2.5mm² twin-and-earth cables incorporating circuit protective conductor or only 1.0mm²

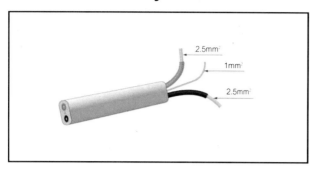

For some years, 2.5mm² twin-and-earth PVC/PVC cables to BS 6004 were manufactured with a circuit protective conductor (cpc) of only 1mm², rather than 1.5mm² as is incorporated today.

The size of the cpc was increased to 1.5mm² in BS 6004 because in certain circumstances the 1mm² cpc may not always be properly protected against thermal effects in the event of an earth fault. This is where the cable is used in a ring final circuit protected by a 30A semi-enclosed (rewirable) fuse. If this is the case, a competent electrician should be consulted about upgrading the cables and/or the consumer unit.

Accessories on wooden mounting blocks

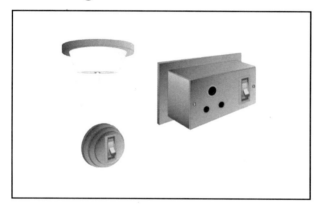

It was commonplace up to the mid-1960s for accessories such as socket-outlets, lighting switches and ceiling roses to be fixed to wooden mounting blocks.

The design of the accessories is often such that the wooden block is used to form part of the enclosure for the unsheathed cores and terminations of cables connecting to the accessory. However, depending on the particular characteristics of the material from which the block is made, it may not satisfy the ignitability requirements of the current Wiring Regulations (BS 7671) for such use.

Cables of imperial (non-metric) sizes

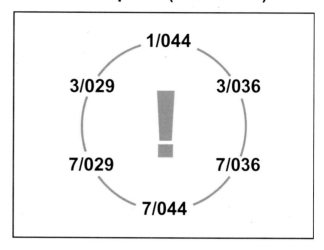

Up until the beginning of the 1970s, cables could still be purchased having imperial, rather than metric, sized conductors. Many such cables are still to be found in older installations.

Their conductors may be single-stranded (as in 1/.044) or may have three, seven or more strands (as in 3/.029, 7/.029 and 19/.044). To the inexperienced eye these cables may be difficult to recognise, other than perhaps by comparison of their conductors with those of metric cables. The important thing to appreciate, however, is that their current-carrying capacity and voltage drop characteristics are likely to be different from those which may at first be expected. It would therefore be prudent to engage a competent electrician to establish whether the performance limits are being exceeded, or would be if a new appliance with a higher rating (e.g. washing machine, dishwasher, towel rail, appliances rated at more than 2kW) were to be connected.

Finally, it should be noted that copper conductors of imperial cables may be of the tinned type, giving them an unfamiliar colour.

Tough rubber-sheathed (TRS), vulcanised rubber insulation (VRI) cables

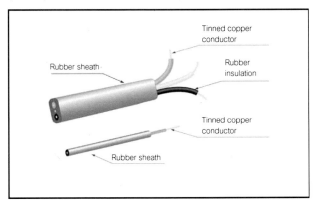

Prior to the use of PVC insulated cables becoming common in the 1960s, most cables installed in domestic dwellings were of the rubber insulated, tough rubber-sheathed (TRS) type. These are easily recognisable by their black exterior.

The extent to which the insulation and sheath deteriorate in service depends very much on whether the cable has been subjected to overloading and/or excessive temperature, or the rubber has been exposed to direct sunlight. Deterioration results in a loss of insulating properties, with the rubber becoming dry and inflexible – perhaps with a tendency to crumble.

Such wiring installations should be tested by a competent person at the earliest opportunity, but otherwise left undisturbed until replacement, as they are beyond their normally expected safe working life.

Lead-sheathed cables

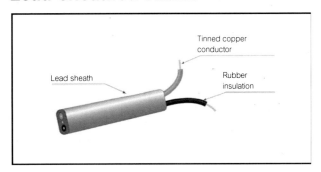

Lead-sheathed cables may be found in some installations dating from before about 1948. These have rubber-insulated, tinned copper conductors and an outer sheath of lead.

For reasons of protection against indirect contact (electric shock) it is essential that the lead sheath of every such cable is, and will remain, properly earthed.

The conductor insulation, being made of rubber, is prone to deterioration as described above for TRS cables.

Again, such wiring installations should be tested by a competent person at the earliest opportunity as they are beyond their normally expected safe working life.

Appendix D: New harmonised cable identification colours

Amendment No 2 to BS 7671:2001 published on 31 March 2004 specifies new (harmonised) cable core colours for all new fixed wiring in electrical installations in the UK. It includes guidance for alterations and additions to installations wired in the old cable colours.

Table D1 gives the new cable core colours for ac power circuits. Figure D1 shows examples of flat and armoured single phase and 3-phase ac power cables with the old and the new harmonised colours.

The new (harmonised) colour cables may be used on site from 31 March 2004. New installations or alterations to existing installations may use either new or old colours, but not both, from 31 March 2004 until 31 March 2006. Only the new colours may be used after 31 March 2006.

For single phase installations in domestic premises, the new colours are the same as those for flexible cables to appliances, namely green-and-yellow, blue and brown for the protective, neutral and phase conductors respectively.

Further information, including cable identification colours for extra-low voltage and dc power circuits, is available from the following sources:

New wiring colours. Leaflet published by the IEE, 2004. Available for downloading from the IEE website at www.iee.org/cablecolours.

ECA comprehensive guide to harmonised cable colours, BS 7671: 2001 Amendment No 2. Electrical Contractors' Association, March 2004.

New fixed wiring colours – A practical guide. National Inspection Council for Electrical Installation Contracting (NICEIC), Spring 2004.

Table D1 Identification of conductors in ac power and lighting circuits

Conductor	Colour
Protective conductor	Green-and-yellow
Neutral	Blue
Phase of single phase circuit	Brown
Phase 1 of 3-phase circuit	Brown
Phase 2 of 3-phase circuit	Black
Phase 3 of 3-phase circuit	Grey

Diagram D1 Examples of cable with old and new colours

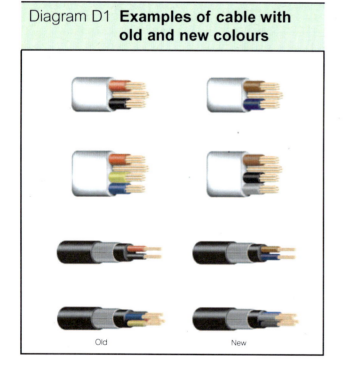

Old   New

Appendix E: Authorised competent person self-certification schemes for electrical installation work

Full scope schemes

The following organisations are authorised to run competent person self-certification schemes for registered electrical installers who can do all types of electrical installation work in dwellings:

BRE Certification Ltd

Bucknalls Lane, Garston, Watford, Herts WD25 9XX
Tel: 0870 609 6093
Website: www.partp.co.uk

British Standards Institution

BSI Product Services, Maylands Avenue, Hemel Hempstead, Herts HP2 4SQ
Tel: 01442 230442
Website: www.bsi-global.com/kitemark

ELECSA Limited

44-48 Borough High Street, London SE1 1XB
Tel: 0870 749 0080
Website: www.elecsa.org.uk

NAPIT Certification Limited

Floor 4, Mill 3, Pleasley Vale Business Park, Outgang Lane, Pleasley Vale, Mansfield, Notts NG19 8RL
Tel: 0870 444 1392
Website: www.napit.org.uk

NICEIC Group Limited

Warwick House, Houghton Hall Park, Houghton Regis, Dunstable, Bedfordshire LU5 6ZX
Tel: 0800 013 0900
Website: www.niceic.org.uk

Defined scope schemes

The following organisations are authorised to run competent person self-certification schemes for registered installers who can do electrical work as an adjunct to or arising out of other work:

CORGI Services Limited

1 Elmwood, Chineham Park, Crockford Lane, Basingstoke, Hants RG24 8WG
Tel: 01256 372200
Website: www.corgi-gas-safety.com

ELECSA Limited

Address and contact details as above

NAPIT Certification Limited

Address and contact details as above

NICEIC Group Limited

Address and contact details as above

OFTEC (Oil Firing Technical Association Limited)

Foxwood House, Dobbs Lane, Kesgrave, Ipswich IP5 2QQ
Tel: 0845 658 5080
Website: www.oftec.co.uk

Standards referred to

BS 7671:2001
Requirements for Electrical Installations (IEE
Wiring Regulations 16th Edition). The Institution of
Electrical Engineers, 2004, ISBN 0 86341 373 0,
(incorporating Amendments No 1:2002 and
No 2:2004).

BS EN 60439-3:1991
Specification for low-voltage switchgear and
controlgear assemblies. Particular requirements
for low-voltage switchgear and controlgear
assemblies intended to be installed in places
where unskilled persons have access to their use.

Other publications referred to

Institution of Electrical Engineers (IEE)

Electrician's guide to the Building Regulations, 2005. ISBN 0 86341 463 X. Available from www.iee.org.

IEE Guidance Note 1: Selection and erection of equipment, 4th edition, 2002. ISBN 0 85296 989 9.

IEE Guidance Note 2: Isolation and switching, 4th edition, 2002. ISBN 0 85296 990 2.

IEE Guidance Note 3: Inspection and testing, 4th edition, 2002. ISBN 0 85296 991 0.

IEE Guidance Note 4: Protection against fire, 4th edition, 2003. ISBN 0 85296 992 9.

IEE Guidance Note 5: Protection against electric shock, 4th edition, 2003. ISBN 0 85296 993 7.

IEE Guidance Note 6: Protection against overcurrent, 4th edition, 2003. ISBN 0 85296 994 5.

IEE Guidance Note 7: Special locations, 2nd edition (incorporating the 1st and 2nd amendments), 2003. ISBN 0 85296 995 3.

IEE On-Site Guide (BS 7671 IEE Wiring Regulations, 16th edition), 2002. ISBN 0 85296 987 2.

New wiring colours, 2004. Leaflet available to download at www.iee.org/cablecolours.

Electrical Contractors' Association (ECA) and National Inspection Council for Electrical Installation Contracting (NICEIC)

ECA comprehensive guide to harmonised cable colours, BS 7671:2001 Amendment No 2, ECA, March 2004.

Electrical Installers' Guide to the Building Regulations, NICEIC and ECA, August 2004. Available from www.niceic.org.uk and www.eca.co.uk.

New fixed wiring colours – A practical guide, NICEIC, Spring 2004.